The Key Facts™ on Taiwan

Taiwan

Essential Information on Taiwan

By Patrick W. Nee

The Internationalist®
www.internationalist.com

The Internationalist®

International Business, Investment, and Travel

Published by:

The Internationalist Publishing Company

96 Walter Street/ Suite 200

Boston, MA 02131, USA

Tel: 617-354-7722

www.internationalist.com

PN@internationalist.com

Copyright © 2014 by PWN

The Internationalist is a Registered Trademark. "Key Facts" and "The Internationalist Business Guides" are Trademarks of The Internationalist Publishing Company.

All Rights are reserved under International, Pan-American, and Pan-Asian Conventions. No part of this book may be reproduced in any form without the written permission of the publisher. All rights vigorously enforced

Table Of Contents

Chapter 1: Background

Chapter 2: Geography

Chapter 3: People and Society

Chapter 4: Government and Key Leaders

Chapter 5: Economy

Chapter 6: Energy

Chapter 7: Communications

Chapter 8: Transportation

Chapter 9: Military

Chapter 10: Transnational Issues

Map of Taiwan

Chapter 1: Background

In 1895, military defeat forced China's Qing Dynasty to cede Taiwan to Japan. Taiwan came under Chinese Nationalist control after World War II. Following the communist victory on the mainland in 1949, 2 million Nationalists fled to Taiwan and established a government using the 1947 constitution drawn up for all of China. Beginning in the 1950s, the ruling authorities gradually democratized and incorporated the local population within the governing structure. This process expanded rapidly in the 1980s. In 2000, Taiwan underwent its first peaceful transfer of power from the Nationalist to the Democratic Progressive Party. Throughout this period, the island prospered and became one of East Asia's economic "Tigers." The dominant political issues continue to be the relationship between Taiwan and China - specifically the question of Taiwan's eventual status - as well as domestic political and economic reform.

Chapter 2: Geography

Location:
>Eastern Asia, islands bordering the East China Sea, Philippine Sea, South China Sea, and Taiwan Strait, north of the Philippines, off the southeastern coast of China

Geographic coordinates:
>23 30 N, 121 00 E

Map references:
>Southeast Asia

Area:
>total: 35,980 sq km
>
>country comparison to the world: 139
>
>land: 32,260 sq km
>
>water: 3,720 sq km

Area - comparative:
>slightly smaller than Maryland and Delaware combined

Land boundaries:
>0 km

Coastline:
>1,566.3 km

Maritime claims:
> territorial sea: 12 nm
> exclusive economic zone: 200 nm

Climate:
> Tropical; marime; rainy season during southwest monsoon (June to August); cloudiness is persistent and extensive all year

Terrain:
> Eastern two-thirds mostly rugged mountains; falt to gently rolling plains in the west

Elevation extremes:
> lowest point: South China Sea 0 m
> highest point: Yu Shan 3,952 m

Natural resources:
> Small deposits of coal, natural gas, limestone, marble, and asbestos

Land use:
> arable land: 24%
> permanent crops: 1%
> other: 75% (2011)

Irrigated land:
> NA

Total renewable water resources:
> 67 cu km (2011)

Natural hazards:

Earthquakes; typhoons

<u>Volcanism:</u> Kueishantao Island (elev. 401 m), east of Taiwan, is its only historically active volcano, although it has not erupted in centuries

Environment - current issues:

Air pollution; water pollution from industrial emissions; raw sewage; contamination of drinking water supplies; trade in endangered species; low-level radioactive waste disposal

Environment - international agreements:

<u>party to</u>: none of the selected agreements because of Taiwan's international status

Geography - note:

Strategic location adjacent to both the Taiwan Strait and the Luzon Strait

Chapter 3: People and Society

Nationality:

noun: Taiwan (singular and plural)

note: example – he or she is from Taiwan; they are from Taiwan

adjective: Taiwan (or Taiwanese)

Ethnic groups:

Taiwanese (including Hakka) 84%, mainland Chinese 14%, indigenous 2%

Languages:

Mandarin Chinese (official), Taiwanese (Min), Hakka dialects

Religions:

Mixture of Buddhist and Taoist 93%, Christian 4.5%, other 2.5%

Population:

23,299,716 (July 2013 est.)

country comparison to the world: 52

Age structure:

0-14 years: 14.3% (male 1,722,887/female 1,609,813)

15-24 years: 13.7% (male 1,638,424/ female 1,549,415)

25-54 years: 47.7% (male 5,562,031/ female 5,553,318)

55-64 years: 12.7% (male 1,450,513/ female 1,509,359)

65 years and over: 11.6% (male 1,262,939/ female 1,441,017) (2013 est.)

Median age:

total: 38.7 years

male: 38 years

female: 39.4 years (2013 est.)

Population growth rate:

0.27% (2013 est.)

country comparison to the world: 171

Birth rate:

8.61/1,000 population (2013 est.)

country comparison to the world: 216

Death rate:

6.83/1,000 population (2013 est.)

country comparison to the world: 140

Net migration rate:

0.91 migrant(s)/1,000 population (2013 est.)

country comparison to the world: 59

Sex ratio:

at birth: 1.07 male(s)/female

0-14 years: 1.07 male(s)/female

15-24 years: 1.06 male(s)/female

25-54 years: 1 male(s)/female

55-64 years: 0.96 male(s)/female

65 years and over: 0.89 male(s)/female

total population: 1 male(s)/female (2013 est.)

Infant mortality rate:

total: 4.55 deaths/1,000 live births

country comparison to the world: 186

male: 4.96 deaths/1,000 live births

female: 4.12 deaths/1,000 live births (2013 est.)

Life expectancy at birth:

total population: 79.71 years

country comparison to the world: 39

male: 76.58 years

female: 83.06 years (2013 est.)

Total fertility rate:

1.11 children born/woman (2013 est.)

country comparison to the world: 222

HIV/AIDS - adult prevalence rate:

NA

HIV/AIDS - people living with HIV/AIDS:
    NA
HIV/AIDS - deaths:
    NA
Education expenditures:
    NA
Literacy:
    <u>definition</u>: age 15 and over can read and write
    <u>total population</u>: 96.1%
    <u>male</u>: NA
    <u>female</u>: NA (2003)

Chapter 4: Government and Key Leaders

Country name:

conventional long form: none

conventional short form: Taiwan

local long form: none

local short form: Taiwan

former: Formosa

Government type:

Multiparty democracy

Capital:

name: Taipei

geographic coordinates: 25 02 N, 121 31 E

time difference: UTC+8 (13 hours ahead of Washington, DC during Standard Time)

Administrative divisions:

includes main island of Taiwan plus smaller islands nearby and off coast of China's Fujian Province; Taiwan is divided into 14 counties (hsien, singular and plural), 3 municipalities (shih, singular and plural), and 5 special municipalities (chih-hsia-shih, singular and plural) note: Taiwan uses a variety of romanization systems; while a modified Wade-Giles system still dominates, the city of Taipei has adopted a Pinyin romanization for street and place names within its boundaries; other local authorities use different romanization systems; names for administrative divisions that follow are taken from the Taiwan Yearbook 2007 published by the Government Information Office in Taipei.

Counties: Changhua, Chiayi (county), Hsinchu (county), Hualien, Kinmen, Lienchiang, Miaoli, Nantou, Penghu, Pingtung, Taitung, Taoyuan, Yilan, Yunlin

Municipalities: Chiayi (city), Hsinchu (city), Keelung (city)

Special municipalities: Kaohsiung (city), New Taipei (city), Taichung (city), Tainan (city), Taipei (city)

National holiday:

Republic Day (Anniversary of the Chinese Revolution), 10 October 1911

Constitution:
> previous 1912, 1931; latest adopted 25 December 1946, promulgated 1 January 1947, effective 25 December 1947; revised several times, last in 2005 (2013)

Legal system:
> Civil law system

International law organization participation:
> Has not submitted an ICJ jurisdiction declaration; non-party state to the ICCt

Suffrage:
> 20 years of age; universal

Executive branch:
> chief of state: President MA Ying-jeou (since 20 May 2008); Vice President WU Den-yih (since 20 May 2012)
>
> head of government: Premier JIANG Yi-huah (President of the Executive Yuan) (since 18 February 2013); Vice Premier MAO Chi-kuo (Vice President of the Executive Yuan) (since 18 February 2013)
>
> cabinet: Executive Yuan - ministers appointed by president on recommendation of premier

elections: president and vice president elected on the same ticket by popular vote for four-year terms (eligible for a second term); election last held on 14 January 2012 (next to be held in January 2016); premier appointed by the president; vice premiers appointed by the president on the recommendation of the premier

election results: MA Ying-jeou elected president; percent of vote - MA Ying-jeou 51.6%, TSAI Ing-wen 45.6%, James SOONG Chu-ye 2.8%

Legislative branch:

unicameral Legislative Yuan (113 seats - 73 district members elected by popular vote, 34 at-large members elected on basis of proportion of islandwide votes received by participating political parties, 6 elected by popular vote among aboriginal populations; members to serve four-year terms); parties must receive 5% of vote to qualify for at-large seats

elections: Legislative Yuan - last held on 14 January 2012 (next to be held in January 2016) election results: Legislative Yuan - percent of vote by party - KMT 44.6%, DPP 34.6%, TSU 9.0%, PFP 5.5%, others 6.3%; seats by party - KMT 64, DPP 40, PFP 3, TSU 3, NPSU 2, independent 1

Judicial branch:

Highest court(s): Supreme Court (consists of the court president, vice president, and approximately 100 judges organized into 8 civil and 12 criminal divisions, each with a division chief justice and 4 associate justices); Constitutional Court (consists of the court president, vice president, and 13 justices)

Judge selection and term of offfice: both Supreme Court and Constitutional Court justices appointed by the president of the republic with the approval of the Legislative Yuan; Supreme Court justices appointed for life; Constitutional Court president, vice-president, and 8 grand justices serve 4-year terms and remaining justices serve 8-year terms

subordinate courts: high courts; district courts; hierarchy of administrative courts

Political parties and leaders:
    Democratic Progressive Party or DPP [SU Tseng-chang]
    Kuomintang or KMT (Nationalist Party) [MA Ying-jeou]
    New Party [YOK Mu-ming]
    Non-Partisan Solidarity Union or NPSU [LIN Pin-kuan]
    People First Party or PFP [James SOONG Chu-ye]
    Taiwan Solidarity Union or TSU [HUANG Kun-huei]

Political pressure groups and leaders:
    Environmental groups

    Independence movement

    Various business groups

    <u>Note:</u> debate on Taiwan independence has become acceptable within the mainstream of domestic politics on Taiwan; public opinion polls consistently show a substantial majority of Taiwan people supports maintaining Taiwan's status quo for the foreseeable future; advocates of Taiwan independence oppose the stand that the island will eventually unify with mainland China; advocates of eventual unification predicate their goal on the democratic transformation of the mainland

International organization participation:
ADB, APEC, BCIE, ICC (national committees), IOC, ITUC (NGOs), WTO

Diplomatic representation in the US:
none; commercial and cultural relations with the people in the United States are maintained through an unofficial instrumentality, the Taipei Economic and Cultural Representative Office in the United States (TECRO), a private nonprofit corporation that performs citizen and consular services similar to those at diplomatic posts

representative: KING Pu-tsung

office4201 Wisconsin Avenue NW, Washington, DC 20016

telephone: [1] (202) 895-1800

Taipei Economic and Cultural Offices (branch offices): Atlanta, Boston, Chicago, Guam, Houston, Honolulu, Kansas City, Los Angeles, Miami, New York, San Francisco, Seattle

Diplomatic representation from the US:
none; commercial and cultural relations with the people on Taiwan are maintained through an unofficial instrumentality, the American Institute in Taiwan (AIT), a private nonprofit corporation that performs citizen and consular services similar to those at diplomatic posts
director: Christopher J. MARUT
office: #7 Lane 134, Hsin Yi Road, Section 3, Taipei 106, Taiwan
telephone: [1] [886] (02) 2162-2000
FAX: [1] [886] (02) 2162-2251
Other offices: Kaohsiung

Flag description:
red field with a dark blue rectangle in the upper hoist-side corner bearing a white sun with 12 triangular rays; the blue and white design of the canton (symbolizing the sun of progress) dates to 1895; it was later adopted as the flag of the Kuomintang Party; blue signifies liberty, justice, and democracy; red stands for fraternity, sacrifice, and nationalism, white represents equality, frankness, and the people's livelihood; the 12 rays of the sun are

those of the months and the twelve traditional Chinese hours (each ray equals two hours)

National symbol(s):

white, 12-rayed sun on blue field

National anthem:

name: "Zhonghua Minguo guoge" (National Anthem of the Republic of China)

lyrics/music: HU Han-min, TAI Chi-t'ao, and LIAO Chung-k'ai/CHENG Mao-Yun

note: adopted 1930; the anthem is also the song of the Kuomintang Party; it is informally known as "San Min Chu I" or "San Min Zhu Yi" (Three Principles of the People); because of political pressure from China, "Guo Qi Ge" (National Banner Song) is used at international events rather than the official anthem of Taiwan; the "National Banner Song" has gained popularity in Taiwan and is commonly used during flag raisings

Chapter 5: Economy

Economy - overview:

Taiwan has a dynamic capitalist economy with gradually decreasing government guidance of investment and foreign trade. Exports, led by electronics, machinery, and petrochemicals have provided the primary impetus for economic development. This heavy dependence on exports exposes the economy to fluctuations in world demand. In 2009, Taiwan's GDP contracted 1.8%, due primarily to a 13.1% year-on-year decline in exports. In 2010 GDP grew 10.7%, as exports returned to the level of previous years, and in 2011, grew 4.0%. In 2012, however, growth fell to 1.3%, because of softening global demand. Taiwan's diplomatic isolation, low birth rate, and rapidly aging population are major long-term challenges. Free trade agreements have proliferated in East Asia over the past several years, but except for the landmark Economic Cooperation Framework Agreement (ECFA) signed with China in June 2010, so far Taiwan has been excluded from this greater economic integration in part because of its diplomatic status. Negotiations continue on such follow-on components of ECFA regarding trade in goods and services. The MA administration has said that the ECFA will serve as a stepping stone toward trade pacts with other key trade partners, which Taiwan subsequently launched with Singapore and New Zealand. Taiwan's Total Fertility rate of just over one child per woman is among the lowest in the world, raising the prospect of future labor shortages, falling domestic demand, and declining tax revenues. Taiwan's population is aging quickly, with the number of people over 65 accounting for 11.2% of the island's total population as of 2012. The island runs a large trade surplus largely because of its surplus with China, and its foreign reserves are the world's fifth largest, behind China, Japan, Saudi Arabia, and Russia. In 2006 China overtook the US to become Taiwan's second-largest source of imports after Japan. China is also the island's number one destination for foreign direct investment. Three financial memorandums of understanding, covering banking, securities, and insurance, took effect in mid-January 2010, opening the island to greater investments from the mainland's financial firms and institutional investors, and providing new opportunities for Taiwan financial firms to operate in China. In August 2012, Taiwan Central Bank signed a memorandum of understanding on cross-Strait currency settlement with its Chinese counterpart. The MOU allows for the direct settlement of Chinese RMB and the New Taiwan dollar across the Strait, which could help develop Taiwan into a local RMB hub. Closer economic links with the mainland bring greater opportunities for the Taiwan economy, but also poses new challenges as the island becomes more economically dependent on China while political differences remain unresolved.

GDP (purchasing power parity):
>$894.3 billion (2012 est.)
>country comparison to the world: 107
>$882.6billion (2011 est.)
>$848.2 billion (2010 est.)
>note: data are in 2012 US dollars

GDP (official exchange rate):
>$467.7 billion (2012 est.)

GDP - real growth rate:
>1.3% (2012 est.)
>country comparison to the world: 152
>4.1% (2011 est.)
>10.8% (2010 est.)

GDP - per capita (PPP):
>$38,400 (2012 est.)
>country comparison to the world: 29
>$38,000 (2011 est.)
>$36,600 (2010 est.)
>note: data are in 2012 US dollars

GDP - composition by sector:
>agriculture: 2%
>industry: 29.8%
>services: 68.2% (2012 est.)

Labor force:
    11.34 million (2012 est.)
    country comparison to the world: 47

Labor force - by occupation:
    agriculture: 5%
    industry: 36.2%
    services: 58.8% (2012)

Unemployment rate:
    4.2% (2012 est.)
    country comparison to the world: 36
    4.4% (2011 est.)

Population below poverty line:
    1.5% (2012 est.)

Household income or consumption by percentage share:
    lowest 10%: 6.4%
    highest 10%: 40.3% (2010)

Distribution of family income - Gini index:
    34.2 (2011)
    country comparison to the world: 91
    32.6 (2000)

Budget:
    revenues: $78.38 billion
    expenditures: $90.42 billion (2012 est.)

Taxes and other revenues:

    16.8% of GDP (2012 est.)

    country comparison to the world: 103

Budget surplus (+) or deficit (-):

    -2.6% of GDP (2012 est.)

    country comparison to the world: 103

Public debt:

    35.8% of GDP (2012 est.)

    country comparison to the world: 105

    34.9% of GDP (2011 est.)

    Note: data for central government

Inflation rate (consumer prices):

    1.9% (2012 est.)

    country comparison to the world: 38

    1.4% (2011 est.)

Central bank discount rate:

    1.88% (31 December 2012)

    country comparison to the world: 113

    1.88% (31 December 2011)

Commercial bank prime lending rate:

    2.88% (31 December 2012 est.)

    country comparison to the world: 177

    2.88% (31 December 2011 est.)

Stock of narrow money:

$426.2 billion (31 December 2012 est.)

country comparison to the world: 13

$390.6 billion (31 December 2011 est.)

Stock of broad money:

$1.119 trillion (31 December 2012 est.)

country comparison to the world: 17

$1.082 trillion (31 December 2011 est.)

Stock of domestic credit:

$743.1 billion (31 December 2012 est.)

country comparison to the world: 19

$692 billion (31 December 2011 est.)

Market value of publicly traded shares:

$831.9 billion (31 December 2012)

country comparison to the world: 18

$784.1 billion (31 December 2011)

$738.3 billion (31 December 2010)

Current account balance:

49.92 billion (2012 est.)

country comparison to the world: 13

$41.23 billion (2011 est.)

Exports:

$299.8 billion (2012 est.)

country comparison to the world: 21

$307 billion (2011 est.)

Exports - commodities:

electronics, flat panels, machinery; metals; textiles, plastics, chemicals; optical, photographic, measuring, and medical instruments

Exports - partners:

China 27.1%, Hong Kong 13.2%, US 10.3%, Japan 6.4%, Singapore 4.4% (2012 est.)

Imports:

$268.8 billion (2012 est.)

country comparison to the world: 20

$279.2 billion (2011 est.)

Imports - commodities:

electronics, machinery, crude petroleum, precision instruments, organic chemicals, metals

Imports - partners:

Japan 17.6%, China 16.1%, US 9.5% (2012 est.)

Reserves of foreign exchange and gold:

$408.5 billion (31 December 2012 est.)

country comparison to the world: 7

$390.6 billion (31 December 2011 est.)

Debt - external:

$130.8 billion (31 December 2012 est.)

country comparison to the world: 41

$122.5 billion (31 December 2011 est.)

Stock of direct foreign investment - at home:

$59.36 billion (31 December 2012 est.)

country comparison to the world: 51

$56.15 billion (31 December 2011 est.)

Stock of direct foreign investment - abroad:

$226.1 billion (31 December 2012 est.)

country comparison to the world: 23

$213.1 billion (31 December 2011 est.)

Exchange rates:

New Taiwan dollars (TWD) per US dollar -
29.616 (2012 est.)
29.47 (2011 est.)
31.648 (2010 est.)
33.061 (2009)
31.53 (2008)

Chapter 6: Energy

Electricity - production:
> 252.2 billion kWh (2011 est.)
>
> country comparison to the world: 17

Electricity - consumption:
> 242.2 billion kWh (2011 est.)
>
> country comparison to the world: 15

Electricity - exports:
> 0 kWh (2011 est.)
>
> country comparison to the world: 141

Electricity - imports:
> 0 kWh (2011 est.)
>
> country comparison to the world: 143

Electricity - installed generating capacity:
> 48.75 million kW (2011 est.)
>
> country comparison to the world: 21

Electricity - from fossil fuels:
> 77.2% of total installed capacity (2011 est.)
>
> country comparison to the world: 94

Electricity - from nuclear fuels:
> 10.6% of total installed capacity (2011 est.)
>
> country comparison to the world: 18

Electricity - from hydroelectric plants:
>5.3% of total installed capacity (2011 est.)
>country comparison to the world: 124

Electricity - from other renewable sources:
>6.9% of total installed capacity (2011 est.)
>country comparison to the world: 34

Crude oil - production:
>21,680 bbl/day (2012 est.)
>country comparison to the world: 75

Crude oil - exports:
>0 bbl/day (2011 est.)
>country comparison to the world: 194

Crude oil - imports:
>885,900 bbl/day (2011 est.)
>country comparison to the world: 13

Crude oil - proved reserves:
>2.38 bbl (1 January 2013 est.)
>country comparison to the world: 95

Refined petroleum products - production:
>920,200 bbl/day (2011 est.)
>country comparison to the world: 22

Refined petroleum products - consumption:
786,100 bbl/day (2011 est.)
>country comparison to the world: 24

Refined petroleum products - exports:
>255,000 bbl/day (2011 est.)

>country comparison to the world: 25

Refined petroleum products - imports:
>304,700 bbl/day (2011 est.)

>country comparison to the world: 20

Natural gas - production:
>330.2 million cu m (2011 est.)

>country comparison to the world: 75

Natural gas - consumption:
>16.37 billion cu m (2011 est.)

>country comparison to the world: 38

Natural gas - exports:
>0 cu m (2011 est.)

>country comparison to the world: 195

Natural gas - imports:
>15.9 billion cu m (2011 est.)

>country comparison to the world: 25

Natural gas - proved reserves:
>6.229 billion cu m (1 January 2012 est.)

>country comparison to the world: 88

Carbon dioxide emissions from consumption of energy:
>293.3million Mt (2011 est.)

>country comparison to the world: 24

Chapter 7: Communications

Telephones - main lines in use:
>15.998 million (2012)
>
>country comparison to the world: 17

Telephones - mobile cellular:
>29.455 million (2012)
>
>country comparison to the world: 35

Telephone system:
>general assessment: provides telecommunications service for every business and private need
>
>domestic: thoroughly modern; completely digitalized
>
>international: country code - 886; roughly 15 submarine fiber cables provide links throughout Asia, Australia, the Middle East, Europe, and the US; satellite earth stations - 2 (2011)

Broadcast media:
>5 nationwide television networks operating roughly 75 TV stations; about 85% of households utilize multi-channel cable TV; national and regional radio networks with about 170 radio stations (2008)

Internet country code:
.tw

Internet hosts:
6.272 million (2012)

country comparison to the world: 18

Internet users:
16.147 million (2009)

country comparison to the world: 24

Chapter 8: Transportation

Airports:
>37 (2013)
>
>country comparison to the world: 107

Airports - with paved runways:
>total: 35
>
>over 3,047 m: 8
>
>2,438 to 3,047 m: 7
>
>1,524 to 2,437 m: 10
>
>914 to 1,523 m: 8
>
>under 914 m: 2 (2013)

Airports - with unpaved runways:
>total: 2
>
>1,524 to 2,437 m: 1
>
>under 914 m: 1 (2013)

Heliports:
>31 (2013)

Pipelines:
>condensate 25 km; gas 802 km; oil 241 km (2013)

Railways:
>total: 1,580 km
>
>country comparison to the world: 86

standard gague: 345 km 1.435-m gauge (345 km electrified)

narrow gague: 1,085 km 1.067-m gauge (685 km electrified); 150 km 0.762-m gauge

note: the 0.762 gauge track belongs to three entities, the Forestry Bureau, the Taiwan Cement and TaiPower (2009)

Roadways:

total: 41,475 km

country comparison to the world: 86

paved: 41,033 km (includes 720 km of expressways)

unpaved: 442 km (2009)

Merchant marine:

total: 112

country comparison to the world: 47

by type: bulk carrier 35, cargo 20, chemical tanker 1, container 31, passenger/cargo 4, petroleum tanker 12, refrigerated cargo 7, roll on/roll off 2

foreign-owned: 3 (France 2, Vietnam 1)

registered in other countries: 579 (Argentina 2, Cambodia 1, Honduras 1, Hong Kong 25, Indonesia 1, Italy 10, Kiribati 2, Liberia 94, Marshall Islands 8, Panama 328, Philippines 1, Sierra Leone 7, Singapore 77, South Korea 1, Thailand 1, UK 11, Vanuatu 1, unknown 8) (2010)

Ports and terminals:

Major seaports: Chilung (Keelung), Kaohsiung, Hualian, Taichung

Chapter 9: Military

Military branches:

Army, Navy (includes Marine Corps), Air Force, Coast Guard Administration, Armed Forces Reserve Command, Combined Service Forces Command, Armed Forces Police Command

Military service age and obligation:

18-35 years of age for compulsory and voluntary military service; service obligation is 2 years; women may enlist; women in Air Force service are restricted to noncombat roles; reserve obligation to age 30 (Army); the Ministry of Defense is in the process of implementing a voluntary enlistment system over the period 2010-2015, although nonvolunteers will still be required to perform alternative service or go through 4 months of military training (2012)

Manpower available for military service:

males age 16-49: 6,183,567
females age 16-49: 6,006,676 (2010 est.)

Manpower fit for military service:

    males age 16-49: 5,074,173

    females age 16-49: 4,951,088 (2010 est.)

Manpower reaching militarily significant age annually:

    male: 166,190

    female: 155,306 (2010 est.)

Chapter 10: Transnational Issues

Disputes - international:

Involved in complex dispute with Brunei, China, Malaysia, the Philippines, and Vietnam over the Spratly Islands, and with China and the Philippines over Scarborough Reef; the 2002 "Declaration on the Conduct of Parties in the South China Sea" has eased tensions but falls short of a legally binding "code of conduct" desired by several of the disputants; Paracel Islands are occupied by China, but claimed by Taiwan and Vietnam; in 2003, China and Taiwan became more vocal in rejecting both Japan's claims to the uninhabited islands of the Senkaku-shoto (Diaoyu Tai) and Japan's unilaterally declared exclusive economic zone in the East China Sea where all parties engage in hydrocarbon prospecting

Illicit drugs:

regional transit point for heroin, methamphetamine, and precursor chemicals; transshipment point for drugs to Japan; major problem with domestic consumption of methamphetamine and heroin; rising problems with use of ketamine and club drugs

Map of Taiwan

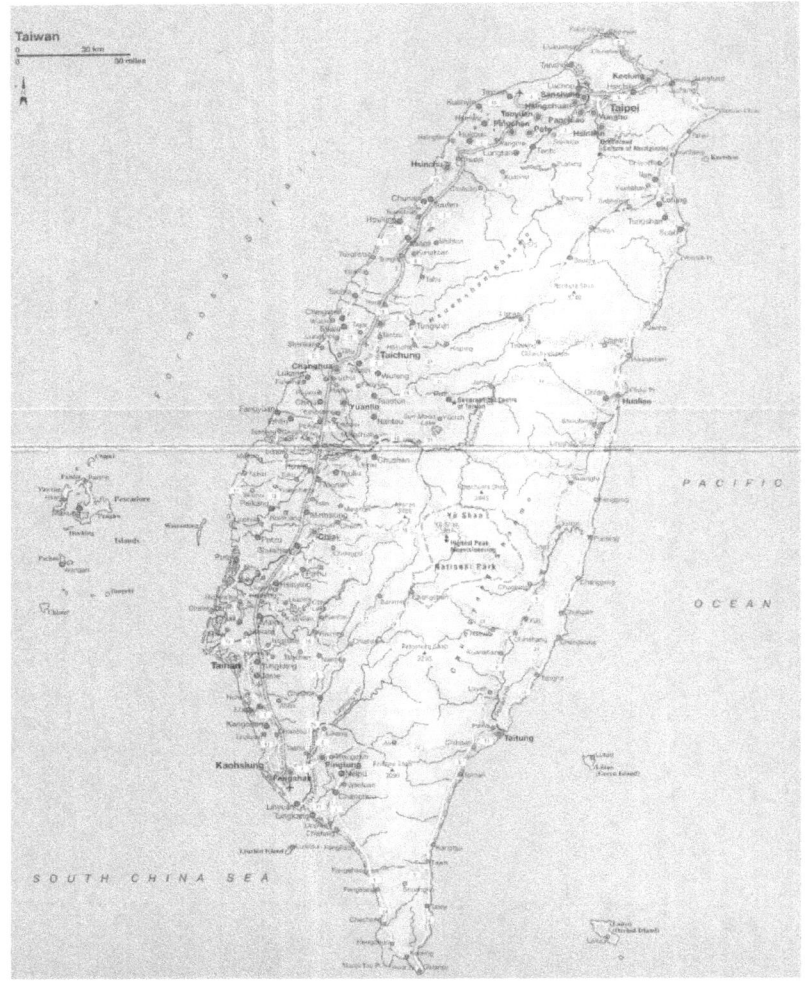

Other Key Facts™ Titles

Key Facts on Syria

Key Facts on China

Key Facts on Qatar

Key Facts on India

Key Facts on Germany

Key Facts on Argentina

Key Facts on Russia

Key Facts on North Korea

Key Facts on Brazil

Key Facts on Italy

Key Facts on the United Arab Emirates

Key Facts on the European Union

Key Facts on Pakistan

Key Facts on Saudi Arabia

Key Facts on Cyprus

Key Facts on Iran

Key Facts on Afghanistan

Key Facts on Iraq

Key Facts on Indonesia

Key Facts on South Korea

Key Facts on France

Key Facts on the United Kingdom

Key Facts on Egypt

Key Facts on Israel

All Key Facts™ Titles are Available at

www.Amazon.com

THE INTERNATIONALIST®
2013
WWW.INTERNATIONALIST.COM

www.ingramcontent.com/pod-product-compliance
Lightning Source LLC
Chambersburg PA
CBHW070716180526
45167CB00004B/1499